PYTHON PROGRAMMING

THE EASIEST PYTHON CRASH COURSE TO GO DEEP THROUGH THE MAIN APPLICATIONS AS WEB DEVELOPMENT, DATA ANALYSIS, AND DATA SCIENCE INCLUDING MACHINE LEARNING

ALAN GRID

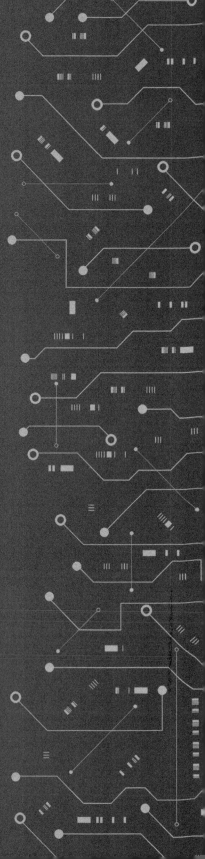

TABLE OF CONTENTS

INTRODUCTION   5

CHAPTER - 1
PYTHON BASICS   15

CHAPTER - 2
CONDITIONAL STATEMENTS   31

CHAPTER - 3
DATA STRUCTURES   39

CHAPTER - 4
DEALING WITH LOCAL VS.
GLOBAL IN PYTHON   55

CHAPTER - 5
MODULES IN PYTHON   63

CHAPTER - 6
OBJECT-ORIENTED
PROGRAMMING
AND FILE HANDLING   73

CHAPTER - 7
DEVELOPMENT TOOLS   85

CHAPTER - 8
PROPER INSTALLATION   95

CHAPTER - 9
DATA SCIENCE   103

CHAPTER - 10
LEARNING MACHINE   113

CONCLUSION   121

INTRODUCTION

The introduction of technologies, especially computers, has influenced our behavior differently. Some people spend most of their time on computers that create programs and websites to make a living, while others mess around with computers to try to understand many different things about how machines work. Programming is one of the areas in networks that most people in the world focus on as a source of income. They can work in a company or computer repair to protect computers from attacks such as hackers or viruses.

One of the most advanced programming tools is Python because anyone, including beginners or experts, can easily use and read it. The secret to using Python is that you can read it because it contains syntax, which allows you as a programmer to express your concepts without necessarily creating a coding page. This is what makes Python easier to use and read than the other codes, including C ++ and Java. Overall, Python is the best language for you because of its usability and readability. We are therefore confident that it will be easy for you to read and understand all the codes you enter while creating your first program during and after this course.

Features of the Python

Python has the following characteristics:

- Large library: it works with other programming projects such as searching for texts, connecting to the web servers, and exchanging files.

- Interactive: Using the Python is very simple because you can easily test codes to determine if they work.

- It is free software; so, you can always download it from the internet with your computer.

- Python programming language can be extended to other modules such as C ++ and C.

- Has an elegant syntax that makes it easy for beginners to read and use.

- Has several basic data types to choose from.

History of the Python

Python programming was discovered by Guido Van Rossum in 1989 while he was carrying out a project at the Dutch research institute CWI, but it was later discontinued. Guido has successfully used a number of basic languages, the so-called ABC language, to work on the Python. According to Van Rossum, the strength of the python language is that you can either keep it simple or extend it to more platforms to support many platforms at once. The design allowed the system to easily communicate with the libraries and various file formats.

Since its introduction, many programmers now use Python in the world, and in fact, many tools are included to improve operation and efficiency. Many programmers have taken various initiatives to educate everyone about using python programming language and how it can help ease the fear of complex computer codes.

However, the Python was made open source by Van Rossum a few years ago to allow all programmers access and even make changes to it. This has changed a lot in the field of programming. For example, there was a release of the Python 2.0. Python 2.0 was community-oriented, making it transparent in the development process. While many people don't use Python, there are still some programmers and organizations that use part of the version.

The Python 3, a unique version, was released in 2008. Although the version has many different functions, it is completely different from the first two versions, and it is not easy to update the program. While this version is not backwards compatible, it has a small creator to show what needs to be changed when uploading the files.

Why you should use Python

There are many types of computer coding programs in the world, each with its advantages and disadvantages. However, Python has proven to be the best option for a variety of reasons, such as readability, and can be used on many platforms without changing things. Using Python has the following advantages;

- Readability

- Since it is designed in the English language, a beginner will find it easy to read and us. There are also a number of rules that help the programmer understand how to format everything, and this makes it easy for a programmer to create a simple code that other people can follow when using their Community

Today, there are many workshops for Python worldwide. A beginner can visit online, offline, or both to learn more or even seek clarification on Python. Also, online and offline workshops can improve your understanding of Python, as well as your socialization skills. It is best for the personal computer as it works successfully on many different platforms. In fact, all beginners find it easy to code or learn from the expert.

- Libraries

For over 25 years, programmers have been using Python to teach the beginners how to use different codes written with it. The system is very open to programmers, and they can use the available codes indefinitely. In fact, a student can download and install the system and use it for their personal use, such as writing your codes and completing the product.

General terms in the Python

Understanding the standard terms used in Python is essential to you. It makes everything easy to know when you get started. Following are the most common terms in the Python programming language;

- Function: Refers to a code block that is called when a programmer uses a calling program. The goal is to also provide free services and accurate calculation.

- Class: A template used for developing user-defined objects. It is friendly and easy to use by everyone, including the beginners.

Ver Immutable: refers to an object with a fixed value and is contained within the code. These can be numbers, strings, or tuples. Such an object cannot be changed.

St Docstring: Refers to a string that is displayed in the function, class definition, and module. This object is always available in the documentation tools.

- List: Refers to the data type built into the Python and contains values sorted. Such values include strings and numbers.

LE IDLE: Stands for an integrated development environment that allows the users to type the code while interpreting and editing it in the same window. Best suited for beginners because it is an excellent example of code.

Interactive: Python has become the most suitable programming language for beginners due to its interactive nature. As a beginner, you can try out many things in the IDLE (interpreter to see their response and effects).

Qu Triple Quoted String: The string helps an individual to have single and double quotes in the string, making it easy to go through different lines of code.

- Object: It refers to all data in a state such as attitudes, methods, defined behaviors, or values.

- Type: Refers to a group of data categories in the programming language and differences in properties, functions, and methods.

- Tuple: Refers to the datatype built into the Python and is an unchanging set of values, although it contains some changeable values.

Advantages of Python Language

Using the Python program has many advantages

over other programming languages such as C ++ and Java. You will be happy to see the availability and how easy it is to learn and use the Python program. Ideally, these are the best programming languages you can use right now, especially if you are a beginner. Following are some of the advantages of using Python language;

- It is easy to use, write and read

Many programmers face some challenges when using programming languages such as Java and C ++. They are difficult to view due to their design. One has to spend a lot of his/her time learning about the use of parentheses, and it is not easy to recognize some of the words used in these programming languages. Such words can scare you, especially if you are just getting acquainted with the programming languages. Unlike Java and C ++ languages, Python does not use crazy brackets. It only uses indents, making it easy to read the page. It uses English, which makes it easy to understand characters.

In addition to using indents, Python uses a lot of white spaces, making it easy to learn and read what's needed. It consists of many places with comments to allow you to understand or get clarification in case the program confuses you. So, check it out, and you will see how easy it is to use the Python programming language.

- It uses English as the primary language

Using Python is easy because the main language is English. As a beginner, you will spend less time reading and understanding the basic words used when programming in Python. So, whether you speak native or non-native English, Python is best for you because most words are simple and easy to understand.

- Python is already available on some computers

Some computers, such as macOS systems and Ubuntu, come with Python pre-installed. In this case, you just need to download the text interpreter to get started with Python programming. However, you must download the program on your computer if you are using a Windows computer. In fact, Python works fine even if you didn't install it from the beginning.

- Python works perfectly with other programming languages

For the first time, you will be using Python alone. However, you will realize that Python can work with other languages as you continue programming. Some of the programming languages that you can work with Python include C ++ and JavaScript. Try to learn more about Python and what it can do practically. You will be able to discover many things over time.

- The Python can be used to test many things

You need to download the test interpreter once you have downloaded the Python. The test interpreter plays an important role in enabling Python to read the information. It's good to use a simple product like Notepad that is available in your Windows or other interpreters.

Disadvantages of using Python programming

While there are many advantages to using Python, it is essential to recognize some of the adverse effects of using it. Some individuals prefer to use other programming languages such as C ++ and JavaScript for Python because of the following negative effects of Python.

• Python has a slow speed

While Python works well with other programming languages and is suitable for beginners, it is unfortunate that Python is not ideal for programmers looking for a high-speed program as it is a slower translated language than the other options. The level of speed depends on the content you are translating because some benchmarks with Python code work faster compared to other codes. Currently, many programmers around the world are trying to solve this problem by making the interpreting speed faster. It is hopeful that Python will run at the same rate or even faster than C and C ++ soon.

• Python is not available in most mobile browsers

While Python works well for those who have regular computers and is accessible on many server platforms and desktops to help individuals create the codes they are looking for, it is not yet ready for mobile computing. Programmers are trying to transition the program to mobile computing to cater to today's large numbers of people who use cell phones.

- Limited design

Python program is not a better option for programmers looking for a program with many design options. For example, the design language is not available in some other options; so, you will need more time to test, and sometimes, a lot of errors can occur when you run the program.

CHAPTER - 1
PYTHON BASICS

Once you have the software installed on your system, it is time to begin your programming adventure with Python. I will start with the fundamentals such as variables, strings, and keywords. Now, you will learn and write your very first program in Python, the different data you can work with, how to use variables, and keywords. Let us begin with the basics to get your coding started right away.

Keywords

async	assert	as	and
def	from	nonlocal	while
continue	for	lambda	try
elif	if	or	yield
else	import	pass	
global	not	with	del
in	raise	false	await
return	none	break	except

| true | class | finally | Is |

Let us begin with the fundamental "Hello" program that is the first step for any programmer.

```
Print ("Hello, Welcome to Python Programming!")
```

When this program code is run, your output will be:

Hello, Welcome to Python Programming!

Python programs always end with the extension .py Let us save this program as Hello.py. Please always remember to save each example using its name in order to recall them when necessary. When you use your editor or IDE, the file is run via the interpreter, which then determines the words used in the program. For instance, in the program below, the interpreter will see the word encircled in parenthesis and prints what is inside the parentheses. In the course of writing Python codes, the editor may highlight certain parts of the program. For instance, it recognizes that print () is a function name and uses a particular color to differentiate it. However, when it gets to the word "Hello Welcome to Python Programming!" it recognizes that it is a Python program code. Therefore, it uses a different color to differentiate it from the other code. This unique feature is known as syntax highlighting and is useful for beginners.

Indentation and Lines

There is nothing like braces to indicate a block of code for function and class in Python. Normally, a block of code is represented by a line indentation that gets enforced in a strong manner. Importantly, the spaces in the indentation vary; however, every statement in the block must have the same amount of indentation. For instance,

```
if False:

    print "False"

else:

    print "True"
```

However, the block of the statement below will generate an error

```
if False:

print "Result"

print "False"

else:

print "Result"

print "True"
```

Consequently, all continuous lines you indent using the same number of spaces will for a block. Let us use another example to show various statement blocks. I will advise you not to try to understand the logic of the program. However, your aim is to understand the various blocks irrespective of their structure.

```
import sys
try:
    # open file stream
    file = open(fileName, "w")
except IOError:
    print "Error when writing to," fileName
    sys.exit()
print "Enter '," fileFinish,
print "' When finished"
while fileText != fileFinish:
    fileText = real_input("Enter text you want: ")
    if fileText == fileFinish:
        # close the file
        file.close
```

```
        break
    file.write(file_text)
    file.write("\n")
file.close()
fileText = real_input("Enter filename: ")
if len(fileName) == 0:
    print "Next time input something"
    sys.exit()
try:
    file = open(fileName, "r")
except IOError:
    print "Error reading file requested"
    sys.exit()
fileText = file.read()
file.close()
print fileText
```

Multiple Line Statements

These statements normally terminate with a new line. Though, it allows you to use a special character (\) to continue a statement. Check the code below:

```
Total_Number = number1 + \
    number2 + \
    number3
```

Notwithstanding, there is an exception to this situation if such statements contain brackets such as (), {}, or []. For instance;

```
months = ['December', 'November,' 'October,'
'September,' 'August,'
            'July,' 'June,' 'May,' 'April,' 'March,'
'February,' 'January']
```

Variables

A variable is a storage location, which has a name assigned to it. In Python, we can assign a value to a variable and recall these variables. I believe an example will make things clearer. Remember our first program (hello.py), let us add an additional two lines. Consider the program below:

```
outcome=   "Hello,   Welcome   to   Python
Programming!"

print(outcome)
```

When you run the program, your output will be the same as the previous one, which was:

Hello, Welcome to Python Programming!

The only difference is that we added a variable called "outcome." Each variable always has a value assigned to it. In this situation, the value of "outcome" is "Hello Welcome to Python Programming!"

Let us add two additional lines to the previous code. However, ensure to insert a blank line in the first code before adding the new codes.

```
outcome=   "Hello,   Welcome   to   Python
Programming!"

print(outcome)

outcome = "Hello, Welcome to Learning Python!"

print(outcome)
```

After adding the two lines, save the file and run the program again. Your output will be as follows:

Hello, Welcome to Python Programming!

Hello, Welcome to Learning Python!

Rules to Variable Naming

There are important rules to adhere to when naming variables in Python. If you break any of these rules, you will get an error message. Therefore, ensure to keep them in your mind when writing your programs.

- Variable names must have only numbers, underscores, and letters. You can begin your variable names with an underscore or a letter; however, it must not begin with a number. For example, your variable name can be outcome_1, but using 1_outcome is completely wrong.

- A variable name must not contain space between them. Notwithstanding, you can use underscores to separate two words. For instance, outcome_program will work; however, the outcome program will cause errors in your program.

- Avoid using function names and keywords as variable names

- Variable names must be short and descriptive when used. For instance, the score is preferable than using s, serial_name is better than sn.

Avoiding Variable Name Errors

As a beginner, you will make mistakes. Professionals aren't exempted from this situation, but they know how to tackle these errors efficiently. Let us look at a more likely mistake you will make as you beginning your Python-programming course. I will intentionally write an error code by misspelling the word "outcome."

```
outcome = "Hello, Welcome to Learning Python!"

#program will generate an error

print(outcom)
```

When such an error occurs, the Python interpreter figures the best way to solve the problem. It provides a traceback once the program cannot run successfully. Not many programming languages have this feature to traceback an error. Let us look at how the interpreter will respond to our program above

Trackback (most recent call last):

1. File "hello.py," line 3, in <module>

2. Print(outcom)

3. NameError: name 'outcome' is not defined

Line 1 reports the presence of an error in line 3 with filename "hello.py" however, the interpreter quickly identifies the error and informs us what particular type of error it is in line 3. In a situation like this, it will signify a name error. Additionally, it will reports that our variable hasn't been properly defined. Whenever you see a name error, it means there is a spelling error, or we didn't set a value to the variable. However, in this example, it was a wrong spelling where we didn't include the letter "e" from our variable name.

```
outcom=  "Hello,  Welcome  to  Python Programming!"

print(outcome)

outcom = "Hello, Welcome to Learning Python!"

print(outcome)
```

The program output will be:

Hello, Welcome to Python Programming!

Hello, Welcome to Learning Python!

You must understand that programming languages are strict; however, they disregard bad and good spellings. Because of this, you don't need to contemplate about grammatical and spelling procedures when creating a variable name.

Exercises to Try

Write a program that intends to perform the following things. Ensure to save the file and following the variable naming rules.

- Write a program that assigns a message to a variable name of your choice and print the message

- In this second program, change the value and use a new message. Then print the message.

- Tick the wrong variable names from the list below

  o   1_school

  o   Fred Love

  o   Fred_love

  o   _exercises

  o   Firsttwoletters

Data Types in Python

When writing codes, we need to store data into memory. These data cannot be stored in the same memory because a number will be different from a letter. For instance, a person's name is alphabetic; address can be alphanumeric characters, whereas age can be stored as a numerical value. Python has data types to define various operations and methods of storing these data types. There are five data types in Python; these are:

- String

- Numbers

- Tuple

- List

- Dictionary

String

This is a series of characters, which is enclosed in quotes. In Python, anything in quotes is regarded as a unique character. Both single and double quotes can be used to form a string in Python.

'Hello World'

"Hello World"

The two statements would produce the same output if we were to run it.

Using Quotes Inside Strings

In Python programming, when using strings, an opening string with a quote must match the ending quote. When you begin a string using a double quotation mark, Python takes the next double quotation mark as the ending of the string. This applies to a single quotation mark.

If you decide to use double quotes inside a string, you have to place them inside single quotes. The example below will show it better.

```
statement = 'Fred is "a boy that lives in New York"'
```

Let's assume you want to use both single and double quotes in a string. In this situation, you have to escape the single, and double quote misses up by using a backslash (\). The example below will demonstrate it.

```
statement_in_single = 'Fred "own\'s a wonderful car in his garage"'

statement_in_double = "Fred\'own's a wonderful car in his garage\""
```

Using Methods to Change Case in String

One simple task you can perform when using strings is to change the case of a particular word. What do you think the output will be for the code below?

```
full_name = "johnson boris"

print(full_name.title())
```

Once you write the code, save the file as name.py before running it. The output will be as follow:

Johnson Boris

If you observe, the variable full_name refers to the string in lowercase "johnson boris." After the variable name comes to the method title().

In Python, a method is an action upon which certain manipulation can be taken on a piece of data. Furthermore, the dot (.) that comes after the variable name informs the interpreter to allow the title() method to interact with our variable name. Parentheses always follow a method because they require additional information to perform their function. The function of the title() method is to change the first letter of each word to capital letter. Furthermore, Python allows us to change string to all lowercase or uppercase.

```
full_name = "Johnson Boris"

print(full_name.lower())

print (full_name.upper))
```

The output will be as follows:

johnson boris

JOHNSON BORIS

Using Variables in Strings

In certain scenarios, you may decide to use a variable, which contains a value in a string. For instance, you may want to use two variables to hold the first name and last name of a person, respectively. Additionally, these two variables must be combined to produce the individual's full name. Let us consider how that is possible in Python.

```
first_name = "johnson"

last_name = "boris"

1.  full_name = f "{first_name} {last_name}"

print(full_name)
```

If you want to insert a variable value to a string, you have to add the letter "f" directly before the opening quotation mark

Consider the code below

```
state = 'United Nation!'    #Assign the variable
"state" to a string 'New York'

print state       # Prints the complete string

print state[0]        # Prints the first character of
the string

print state[0:4]       # Prints characters starting
from 1st to 4th

print state[3:]    # Prints string starting from 4th
character

print state * 3     # Prints string three times

print state + "United State" # Prints concatenated
string
```

The output will be –

United Nation!

U

United

Nations!

United Nation! United Nation!

United Nation! United State

CHAPTER - 2

CONDITIONAL STATEMENTS

Now, it is time to move on to the topic of conditional statements, which can also go by the name of decision control statements. These are going to be the statements that allow the computer to make some decisions based on the input that the user has, as well as what you would like to happen with the program. You will have many times in your program where you will want the computer to make some decisions and complete itself when you are not there. If you are working on a code where you would like the user to put in their answer, rather than giving them two options to work with, then these decision control statements are going to be good options to work with.

There are going to be a few different options that you can work with when you are making these conditional statements. The three most common ones are going to include the if statement, the if-else statement, and the elif statement. As a beginner, we are going to start with the basics of the if statement to get a good idea of how these can work, and then we will build up to understand some of the more complicated things that you can do with these conditional statements.

The first option that we are going to take a look at is the if statement. The if statement is going to work with the ideas, and the answer that your user gives to the computer is going to be either true or false. If the user does an input of information that is seen as true based on your code, then the interpreter can continue with the program, and it will show up the statements or the information that you would like. But, if the user is on the program and puts in something that doesn't match up with your code, and is seen as false, then the program is automatically going to end.

The good news is that we can go through a bit later, and look at the steps that you can take to ensure that you are going to get the program to respond no matter what answer your user gives, but that is not what the if statement is going to focus on. We need to take a look at this simplified form for now, and then build up from there. To help us look at how the if statement is meant to look when your user interacts with it, you will need to work with the following code:

```
age = int(input("Enter your age:"))

if (age <=18):

print("You are not eligible for voting, try next election!")

print("Program ends")
```

Once you have added this conditional statement to your compiler, we need to explore what is going to happen with the above code. If the user does come to this part of the program, and they say that they are under the age of 18, then there will be a message that comes up on the screen. In this case, we wrote in that the message that will come up is going to be, "You are not eligible for voting, try next election!" Then the program, because we don't have any other parts of the code here right now, is going to end. But, this brings up the question of what is going to happen with this particular code if the user does say that they are older than 18?

When a computer programmer is working with the if statement, if the user puts their age in at over 18, then nothing is going to happen. The if statement is going to be the option that you use when you only want the user to pick out the one answer that your code says is true. The user has to say that they are younger than 18 in this situation, or the program is going to be done.

As you can imagine here, this is going to cause us some problems. You most likely would want to allow your user to put in any age that works for them. Some of the users who will come to this program are going to be older than 18, and you don't want the program to end without anything there because they are older than that age range. This is going to end the program before you want it to, and it doesn't look that professional with the program that you are working with when the code ends. This is a big reason why you are not going to see the if statements all that often.

But this is where we are going to bring in the if-else statements and use those to fix this problem. These take the idea that we were going through, the issues that we brought up, and helping us to deal with them. Let's say that you are working with the code that we had before, and you want to make sure that your program brings up a result, no matter what answer the user decides to put into the program. You can write out an if-else statement so that you can get an answer for those who are under the age of 18, and then a different answer for those who are 18 and older. The code for this expands out the option that we talked about before, but here is an example that you can use.

```
age = int(input("Enter your age:"))
```

```
if (age <=18):

print("You are not eligible for voting, try next election!")

else

print("Congratulations! You are eligible to vote. Check out your local polling station to find out more information!)

print("Program ends")
```

This code is going to be a lot more useful to your endeavors and what you want to happen in your code, and it provides you with some more options than before. And the best part is that your code is not going to end because the user puts in their age. It is going to provide them with a statement on the screen based on the age that they put into it.

This code can also be expanded out to include some more possibilities if you would like. The example above just had two options, those under the age of 18 and those above. But you can have more options if it works for your program. For example, you can split up the age ranges a bit more if you would like. Maybe you want to know who is under the age of 18, who is in their 20's, who is in their 30's, and those who are older than 40. You can use this same idea and add in some more lines to it, to help meet the needs of your program using the if-else statement.

Another example that you may want to use when it comes to the if-else statement is when you ask the program to pick out their favorite color. You probably do not want to go through and write out enough code to handle each color that is out there in the world, but you will leave this open so that the user can put in the information that corresponds with their favorite color.

For this code, you may choose to have a list of six colors that you write out in the code (you can have more or less for what you need), and then you will have a message that corresponds to these six colors. You may pick out the colors of yellow, orange, green, blue, purple, and red. Then, you can add an else statement so that the user can pick out a different color. If the user decides to have white as their favorite color here, then the seventh, and the final message will come up. This final message is going to be the same for any of the colors that don't fit in with the original six.

Adding this else statement, or the catch-all, to the end of the code can be an important thing that you need to consider. You can't possibly list out all of the different colors that your user may choose to work with. You may take the time to put in a hundred different colors (but this takes a lot of time and code, and you won't want to do this), but then the user could go with the one color that you forget. If you don't add this else statement to the end, then the program is going to be lost at how you would like it to behave here.

The else statement is nice because it is going to be the one that you can use to catch more than one result from the user, and it can catch all of the answers that you don't account for, but that the user may choose to use. If you don't add a statement in the code, then your program isn't going to be sure how to behave when the user puts that answer in.

The Elif Statements

The other two options of conditional statements are going to be important for a lot of the codes that you would like to work with. The if statement is a good one to learn as a beginner getting into these statements, and they will help you to mostly get a good idea of how the conditional statements are supposed to work. These if statements are going to have a basis on the idea of the answer being either true or false.

In this case, if the answer received from the user is seen as true based on the conditions that you add to the code, then the program will see this and continue on its path. But if the condition is seen to be false, then the program is not going to have anything set up, and it is going to end. This is a simple idea to work with and is a good way to learn more about the conditional statements, but for many of the codes that you want to write out in Python, it is not going to give you the results that you want.

Then we took a look at the if-else statements. These took this idea a bit further, and it understood that the ideas that come with the original if statements are going to be too simple. These if-else statements can help us handle any answer that the user will give to the system, and ensure that the program doesn't just stop. We even took a look at an example code that shows us how these kinds of statements work.

From here, we need to spend some time working on the elif statements. This is going to handle things a bit different than what the other two did, but it is still going to be useful and can add an element of fun and something different to your code. The elif statement is going to give the user a chance to pick from a few options that you present to them. And then, the answer that the user chooses is going to provide them with a predetermined statement that you added into the code.

There are different places where you can see these conditional statements. The elif statement is a unique code for the Python language, and it is often going to be used for many games, or for a different program that you would like to have with the menu style of choices for the user. These statements are going to be used most often if the computer programmer would like to provide their user with some options rather than just one or two.

CHAPTER - 3
DATA STRUCTURES

Python is based on three reference structures: tuples, lists, and dictionaries. These structures are actually objecting that may contain other objects. They have quite different utilities and allow you to store information of all types.

These structures have a number of common features:

To extract one or more objects from a structure, we always use the []

For numerically indexed structures (tuples and lists), the structures are indexed to 0 (the first position is position 0)

The Tuples

This is a structure that groups multiple objects in indexed order. Its form is not modifiable (immutable) once created and is defined using parentheses. It has only one dimension. Any type of object can be stored in a tuple. For example, if you want to create a tuple with different objects, we use:

```
tup1 = (1, True, 7.5.9)
```

You can also create a tuple by using the tuple () function. Access to the values of a tuple is done by the classical indexing of structures. Thus, if we want to access the third element of our tuple, we use:

```
In []: tup1 [2]

Out []: 7.5
```

Tuples can be interesting because they require little memory. Else, on the other hand, they are used as outputs of functions returning several values. Tuples as structures are objects. They have methods that are clean. These are few for a tuple:

```
In []: tup1.count (9)

Out []: 1
```

We often prefer lists that are more flexible.

Lists

The list is the reference structure in Python. It is modifiable and can contain any object.

Creating a list

We create a list using square brackets:

```
list1 = [3,5,6, True]
```

You can also use the list () function. The structure of a list is editable. It has many methods:

.append (): add value at the end of the list

.insert (i, val): insert value to the index i

.pop (i): retrieves the value of the index i

.reverse (): reverse the list

.extend (): extends the list with a list of values

Note—All of these methods modify the list, the equivalent in terms of classic code would be the following:

```
liste1.extend (list2)

equivalent to
```

```
list1 = list1 + list2
```

Lists have other methods including:

.index (val): returns the index of the value val

.count (val): returns the number of occurrences of val

.remove (val): remove the first occurrence of the value val from the list

Extract an Item from a List

As we have seen above, it is possible to extract an element using the brackets:

```
list1 [0]
```

We are often interested in the extraction of several elements. It is done by using the two points:

```
list1 [0: 2] or list1 [: 2]
```

In this example, we see that this system extracts two elements: the indexed element in 0 and the one indexed in position 1. So we have as a rule that i: j goes from the element I included in element j not included. Here are some other examples:

```
# Extract the last element

list1 [-1]

Extract the last 3 elements list1 [-3: -1] or list1 [-3:]
```

A concrete example

Suppose we wanted to create a list of countries. These countries are ordered in the list according to their population. We will try to extract the first three and the last three.

```
In []: country_list = ["China," "India," "United States," "France," "Spain," "Swiss"]

In []: print (country_list [: 3])

['China', 'India', 'United States']

In []: print (country_list [-3:])

['France', 'Spain', 'Switzerland']

In []: country_list.reverse ()

print (liste_pays)

['Switzerland', 'Spain', 'France', 'United States', 'India', 'China']
```

The Comprehension Lists

These are lists built iteratively. They are often very useful because they are more efficient than using loops to build lists. Here is a simple example:

```
In []: list_init = [4,6,7,8]

list_comp = [val ** 2 for val in list_init if val% 2 == 0]
```

The list comp_list allows you to store the even elements of list_init set to the square.

We will have:

```
In []: print (list_comp)

[16,36,64]
```

This notion of comprehension list is very effective. It avoids useless code (loops on a list) and performs better than creating a list iteratively. It also exists in dictionariesbutnotontuplesthatareunchangeable. We will be able to use comprehension lists in the framework of the manipulation of data tables.

Strings—Character Lists

Strings in Python are encoded by default (since Python 3) in Unicode. You can declare a string of characters in three ways:

```
string1 = "Python for the data scientist"

string2 = 'Python for the data scientist'

string3 = "" "Python for the data scientist" ""
```

The last one allows having strings on several lines. We will most often use the first. A string is actually a list of characters, and we will be able to work on the elements of a string as on those of a list:

```
In []: print (string1 [: 6])

print (string1 [-14:])

print (string1 [3:20 p.m.])
```

Python for the Data Scientist

Data strings can be easily transformed into lists:

In []: # we separate the elements using space

```
list1 = chaine1.split ()

print (list1)

['Python', 'for', 'the', 'Data', 'Scientist']

In []: # we join the elements with space

string1bis = "" .join (list1)
```

```
print (chaine1bis)
```

Dictionaries

The dictionaries constitute a third central structure to develop in Python. They allow key-value storage. So far, we have used items based on numerical indexing. So in a list, you access an element using its position list1 [0]. In a dictionary, we will access an element using a key defined when creating the dictionary. We define a dictionary with braces:

dict1 = {"cle1": value1, "cle2": value2, "cle3": value3}

This structure does not require any homogeneity of type in the values. From this, we can have a list like value1, a boolean like value2, and an integer a value3.

To access an element of a dictionary, we use:

```
In []: dict1 ["cle2"]

Out []: value2
```

To display all the keys of a dictionary, we use:

```
In []: dict1.keys

Out []: ("cle1," "cle2," "cle3")
```

To display all the values of a dictionary, we use:

```
In []: dict1.items ()

Out []: (value1, value2, value3)
```

One can easily modify or add a key to a dictionary:

```
In []: dict1 ["key4"] = value4
```

You can also delete a key (and the associated value) in a dictionary:

```
In []: del dict1 ["cle4"]
```

As soon as you are more experienced in Python, you will use more dictionaries. At first, we tend to favor lists dictionaries because they are often more intuitive (with numerical indexing). However, more expert Pythonist will quickly realize the usefulness of dictionaries. In particular, we will be able to store the data as well as the parameters of a model in a very simple way. Plus, the flexibility of Python's for loop adapts very well to dictionaries and makes them very effective when they are well built.

Programming

The Conditions

A condition in Python is very simple to implement; it is a keyword. As mentioned before, the Python language is based on the indentation of your code. We will use an offset for this indentation with four spaces. Fortunately, tools like Spyder or Jupyter notebooks will automatically generate this indentation.

Here is our first condition, which means "if a is true, then display" it is "true":

if a is True:

```
print ("it's true")
```

There is no exit from the condition; it is the indentation that will allow to manage it. Generally, we are also interested in the complement of this condition; we will use else for that:

if a is True:

```
print ("it's true")
else:
print ("it's not true")
```

We can have another case if our variable a is not necessarily a boolean, we use elif:

if a is True:

```
print ("it's true")

elif a is False:

print ("it's wrong")

else:

print ("it's not a boolean")
```

The Loops

Loops are central elements of most programming languages. Python does not break this rule. However, you must be very careful with an interpreted language such as Python. Indeed, the treatment of loops is slow in Python, and we will use it in loops with few iterations. We avoid creating a loop repeating itself thousands of times on the lines of an array of data. However, we can use a loop on the columns of a data table to a few dozen columns.

The for loop

The Python loop has a somewhat specific format; it is a loop on the elements of a structure. We will write:

```
for elem in [1, 2]:
```

```
print (elem)
```

This piece of code will allow you to display 1 and 2. So the iterator of the loop (elem in our case) thus takes the values of the elements of the structure in the second position (after the in). These elements may be in different structures, but lists will generally be preferred.

Range, zip and enumerate functions

These three functions are very useful functions, they make it possible to create specific objects that may be useful in your code for your loops. The range () function is used to generate a sequence of numbers, starting from a given number or 0 by default and up to a number not included:

```
In []: print (list (range (5)))

[0, 1, 2, 3, 4]

In []: print (list (range (2,5)))

[2, 3, 4]

In []: print (list (range (2,15,2)))

[2, 4, 6, 8, 10, 12, 14]
```

We see here that the created range object can be easily transformed into a list with the list ().

In a loop, this gives:

```
for i in range (11):

print (i)
```

The zip and enumerate functions are also useful functions in loops and they use lists.

The enumerate () function returns the index and the element of a list. If we take our list of countries used earlier:

```
In []: for i, in enumerate (country_list):

print (i, a)
```

1. Swiss

2. Spain

3. France

4. United States

5. India

6. China

The zip function will allow linking many lists and simultaneously iterating elements of these lists.

If, for example, we want to simultaneously increment days and weather, we may use:

```
In []: for day, weather in zip (["Monday," "Tuesday"], ["beautiful," "bad"]):

print ("% s, it will make% s"% (day.capitalize (), weather))
```

Monday, it will be nice

Tuesday, it will be bad

In this code, we use zip () to take a pair of values at each iteration. The second part is a manipulation of the character strings. If one of the lists is longer than the other, the loop will stop as soon as it arrives at the end of one of them.

We can link enumerate and zip in one code, for example:

```
In []: for i, (day, weather) in enumerate (zip (["Monday," "Tuesday"], ["good," "bad"])):

print ("% i:% s, it will make% s"% (i, day.capitalize (), meteo))
```

0: Monday, it will be nice

1: Tuesday, it will be bad

We see here that i is the position of the element i.

Note—Replace in a string.

While loop

Python also allows you to use a while () loop that is less used and looks a lot like the while loop that we can cross in other languages. To exit this loop, we can use a station wagon with a condition. Warning, we must increment the index in the loop, at the risk of being in a case of an infinite loop.

We can have:

```
i = 1

while i <100:

i + = 1

if i> val_stop:

break

print (i)
```

This code adds one to i to each loop and stops when i reaches either val_stop, that is 100.

Note—The incrementation in Python can take several forms i = i + 1 or i + = 1.

Both approaches are equivalent in terms of performance; it's about choosing the one that suits you best.

CHAPTER - 4

DEALING WITH LOCAL VS. GLOBAL IN PYTHON

Now we need to take a look at some of the different types of variables that you are able to work with when it is time to handle them in Python. The two main types of variables that we are going to work within this language will include the local variable and the global variable.

There are some big differences that are going to show up when we are talking about these variables. To start with is the global variable. This is mainly going to mean that we are looking at a variable that the rest of the program, or any part of the program, is able to declare. It doesn't matter where that part of the program is located; it will be able to use and rely on that global variable when it would like to.

Sometimes this is a good thing and will allow your modules to declare the variables that they want, even when they are not near one another. But other times, this is going to cause some issues. If the wrong part of the code tries to declare some of the variables that it shouldn't, it can cause the code to not behave the way that you want, and some of the variables are going to get declared at the wrong time. This is never a good thing, and it is going to require you to take some chances if you want to avoid this issue.

The solution to this issue is going to be the local variables. These are the ones that can't be accessed throughout the code. These are the variables that are only going to be declared in a specific method or function that you determine ahead of time. This will make sure that the variable is going to only be used in the manner that you would like, and nowhere else.

The Local Variable

The first option that we are going to take some time to look at is the local variable. This is going to be similar to what we will see with a local variable in other languages, and it is going to be the one that is declared at the beginning of the block that the variable is supposed to be local to at that time. It can also show up when we are working with a statement, a switch statement, and more depending on your needs.

The local variable is going to have a declaration with it that can explicitly define the type of the variable that has been declared along with some of the identifiers that will name out the variable at the same time. We will recognize the local variable as a type of variable that we are able to use where the scope and the extent of the variable are within the method or the statement block in which it is declared.

We are able to use these local variables more like an iteration variable in the foreach statement, the exception variable in the specific catch clause, and the resource variable when we are doing the using statement. It can also be used as a type of constant whose value can't be modified within the method or the statement block in which we declare it.

A local variable that is implicitly typed whose type is going to be inferred by the computer from the expression on its right is going to be useful when you would like to deal with the language-integrated queries. These are going to be the types of queries that will return to us some anonymous types in creating a custom type for each of the sets of results that you have.

The memory allocation that you are going to find with this kind of a variable is often going to be based on the type of variable that you are working with. If you are working with something like an integer or a structure, then the entirety of the contents will be stored in a stack. But if you are using a reference type of variable, it is going to be placed in the reference portion of the stack, and the contents will be in the heap that goes with it.

A local variable is one that needs to not be referred to in the code in any kind of textual position that will proceed with the declaration statement of your local variable. In addition, we have to remember that when we are in one single block, there can never be more than one variable that has the same name. Doing this is going to be a bad thing because it is going to cause an error to show up and will basically just confuse the code that you are working with. However, multiple local variables of the same type can be declared, and it can be initialized, in one single statement.

Within the method of a class that you find one of these local variables and it is named in a manner that is similar to its field, you will find that the local variable is going to hide the field while still being able to access it within the method. It is often more efficient for us to work with a local variable rather than a field.

Looking at a Global Variable

The other thing that we need to take a look at here is what a global variable is all about. This is going to be a type of variable that we will declare outside of any of our functions, which means that it is easy to access by all of the functions that are found in the program that you are writing. A group of these variables is called a global environment or a global state, because when they are combined, and they are going to define various aspects of a program or an environment when the program is going to run.

A global variable is going to be the one that is declared on top of all the other functions, and it is usually best if we can keep this to a minimum. This is because all of the functions will be able to manipulate these variables during the run time of the program. For most of the programs that you want to handle in this language, this can be dangerous because there is the possibility that they can be changed on accident, and that causes bugs in the system.

Global variables, as we can guess by the name, will be some variables that we can access globally, or everywhere throughout the program. Once we go through the process of declaring them, these are going to stay in the memory throughout the runtime of the program. This means that we are able to get them changed with any function that we want, at any time when the program is running, and this can definitely cause some issues with the program as a whole.

During some of the earlier years when computers can be used, but they had a limited amount of memory, these global variables were seen as bad practice because they would take up a lot of valuable information and memory, and it was easier for the programmer to start losing track of the values they worked with, especially in longer programs. And basically, it brought in a lot of bugs to the program that was hard to locate and fix.

Source code is always going to be easier to use and to understand when the scope of its elements is limited. This is something that is hard to do when we are working with the global variables because they are not local, and it becomes really hard to figure out and see where these variables have been changed or even the reason why they were changed in the first place.

Even with this kind of stigma, these global variables are going to be pretty valuable when we are working in functions that do not chare a relation that is known as caller and called. This means that the function is not going to have signal handlers or any kind of concurrent threads. With the exception of those global variables that are declared as read-only values in the protected memory, the codes need to make sure they are able to deploy some of the proper encapsulation in order to be seen as thread-safe in the process.

As we can see here, there are some benefits, and even some negatives, that come with working on this kind of variable. There are still some uses of working with this, which is why we spent some time taking a look at them and figuring out why they are important, but for the most part, the local variables are better and will keep some more control in the codes that you are writing.

Putting It All Together

This may seem a bit confusing in the beginning, but the good news is that there are a number of things that we are able to do when it is time to work with these two variables. And to help us gain a better understanding of the differences between global and local variables with the program that we used below:

1. The variable "f" is going to be one that has a global scope, and it is going to be assigned value 101, which is printed in the output.

2. The variable f is also going to be declared in a function and assumes local scope. It is going to be assigned to a value, and in this case, it is going to be assigned to a value "I am learning Python." Which is going to then be printed out as an output. This variable is different from that global variable f that we tried to define in the previous step.

3. Once we have been able to call the function over, the local variable f is going to be destroyed. At line 12, when we again go through and print off the value off, it is going to show us the global variable that is f = 101.

We can then go through and use the keyword of global, and this will make sure that we are then able to reference the variable that is global inside of the function. Some of the things that we are going to be able to follow with this one will include:

1. The variable "f" is going to be global with its scope, and then it is going to be given a value of 101, which is going to be printed as the output.

2. This same variable is going to be declared when we use the global keyword. This is not going to be the local variable here, but the same global variable that we were able to declare earlier. This means that when we go through and print out the value, the output that we get is going to be 101.

3. We then went and changed the value of 'f" inside of the function. Once we are done with the function call, the changed value of the variable "f" will persist. At line 12, when we again go through and print off the value of "f," the value that we are going to get here is "changing a global variable."

There are a lot of times when you will be able to use the idea of the global and local variables that you would like to handle. Knowing how each of these is going to work, and when each one is going to be the most important part of working with these when you would like them.

CHAPTER - 5

MODULES IN PYTHON

What are the Modules?

In Python, a module is a portion of a program (an extension file) that can be invoked through other programs without having to write them in every program used. Besides, they can define classes and variables. These modules contain related sentences between them and can be used at any time. The use of the modules is based on using a code (program body, functions, variables) already stored on it called import. With the use of the modules, it can be observed that Python allows simplifying the programs a lot because it allows us to simplify the problems into a smaller one to make the code shorter so that programmers do not get lost when looking for something in hundreds of coding lines when making codes.

How to Create a Module?

To create a module in Python, we don't need a lot; it's very simple.

For example: if you want to create a module that prints a city, we write our code in the editor and save it as "mycity.py."

Once this is done, we will know that this will be the name of our module (omitting the .py sentence), which will be assigned to the global variable __city__.

But, beyond that, we can see that the file "mycity.py" is pretty simple and not complicated at all, since the only thing inside is a function called "print_city" which will have a string as a parameter, and what it will do is to print "Hello, welcome to," and this will concatenate with the string that was entered as a parameter.

Locate a Module

When importing a module, the interpreter automatically searches the same module for its current address, if this is not available, Python (or its interpreter) will perform a search on the PYTHONPATH environment variable that is nothing more than a list containing directory names with the same syntax as the environment variable.

If in any particular case, these previous actions failed, Python would look for a default UNIX path (located in /user/local/lib/python on Windows).

The modules are searched in the directory list given by the variable sys.path.

This variable contains the current directory, the PYTHONPATH directory, and the entire directory that comes by default in the installation.

Import Statement

This statement is used to import a module. Through any Python code file, its process is as follows: The Python interpreter searches the file system for the current directory where it is executed. Then, the interpreter searches for its predefined paths in its configuration.

When it meets the first match (the name of the module), the interpreter automatically executes it from start to finish. When importing a module for the first time, Python will generate a compiled .pyc extension file. This extension file will be used in the following imports of this module. When the interpreter detects that the module has already been modified since the last time it was generated, it will generate a new module.

You must save the imported file in the same directory where Python is using the import statement so that Python can find it.

As we could see in our example, importing a module allows us to improve the functionalities of our program through external files.

Now, let's see some examples. The first one is a calculator where will create a module that performs all the mathematical functions and another program that runs the calculator itself.

The first thing we do is the module "calculator. py" that is responsible for doing all the necessary operations. Among them are the addition, subtraction, division, and multiplication, as you can see.

We included the use of conditional statements such as if, else, and elif. We also included the use of exceptions so that the program will not get stuck every time the user enters an erroneous value at the numbers of the calculator for the division.

After that, we will create a program that will have to import the module previously referred to so that it manages to do all the pertinent mathematical functions.

But at this time, you might be thinking that the only existing modules are the ones that the programmer creates. The answer is no since Python has modules that come integrated to it.

With them, we will make two more programs: the first one is an improvement of the one that we have just done, and the second one will be an alarm that will print on screen a string periodically.

Example:

Create a python module called dummymodule.py and write the following inside

```
def testF():

    print("this is a module, goodbuy")
```

save the module in the python installation directory.

In the shell

Import dummymodule

Now call the function

```
dummymodule.testF()
```

You have used your first module.

Module example One

The first thing that was done was to create the module, but at first sight, we have a surprise, which is that math was imported.

What does that mean to us?

Well, that we are acquiring the properties of the math module that comes by default in Python.

We see that the calculator function is created that has several options.

If the op value is equal to 1, the addition operation is made.

If it is equal to 2, the subtraction operation is made, and so on.

But so new is from op is equal to 5 because, if this is affirmative, then it will return the value of the square root of the values num1 and num2 through the use of math.sqrt(num1), which returns the result of the root.

Then, if op is equal to 6, using functions "math. radians()," which means that num1 or num2 will become radians since that is the type of value accepted by the functions "math.sin()," meaning that the value of the sin of num1 and num2 will return to us, which will be numbers entered by users arbitrarily who will become radians and then the value of the corresponding sin.

The last thing will be to create the main program, as it can be seen next:

Here, we can see the simple program, since it only imports the module "calculator.py," then the variables num1 and num2 are assigned the value by using an input.

Finally, an operation to do is chosen, and to finish is called the calculator function of the calculator module to which we will pass three parameters.

Module example Two

We are going to create a module, which has within itself a function that acts as a chronometer in such a way that it returns true in case time ends.

In this module, as you can see, another module is imported, which is called as "time," and as its name refers, functions to operate with times, and has a wide range of functions, from returning dates and times to help to create chronometers, among others.

The first thing we do is to create the cron() function, which starts declaring that the start Alarm variables will be equal to time.time, which means that we are giving an initial value to this function o know the exact moment in which the function was initialized to then enter into an infinite cycle.

Since the restriction is always True, therefore, this cycle will never end, unless the break command is inside it.

Then, within the while cycle, there are several instructions.

The first is that the final variable is equal to time. time() to take into account the specific moment we are located and, therefore, to monitor time.

After that, another variable is created called times, and this acquires the value of the final minus start Alarm.

But you will be wondering what the round function does. It rounds up the values; we do that to work easier. But this is not enough; therefore, we use an if since, if the subtraction between the end and the beginning is greater or equal to 60, then one minute was completed, and what happens to this?

Why 60?

This is because the time module works with a second and for a minute to elapse, 60 seconds have to be elapsed; therefore, the subtraction between the end and the beginning has to be greater than or equal to 60, in the affirmative case, True will be returned, and finally, we will get out of the infinite cycle.

Once the alarm module is finished, we proceed to make the program, as we can see below:

We can see that the program imports two modules, the one we have created, the alarm and the time module.

The first thing we do is to create the variable s as an input, which tells the user if he wants to start.

If the answer is affirmative, then the variable h representing the time will be equal to "time. strftime ("%H:%M:%S")," which means that we are using a function of the time module that returns the hour to use in the specified format so that it can then be printed using the print function.

The next action is to use the alarm module using the command alarm.cron(), which means that the cron() function is being called.

When this function is finished, the time will be assigned to the variable h, again, to finish printing it and being able to observe its correct operation.

As a conclusion of this chapter, we can say that the modules are fundamental for the proper performance of the programmer since they allow to make the code more legible, in addition, that it allows subdividing the problems to attack them from one to one and thus to carry out the tasks easily.

CHAPTER - 6

OBJECT-ORIENTED PROGRAMMING AND FILE HANDLING

Object-Oriented programming is an extensive concept used to create powerful applications. Data scientists are required to build applications to work on data, among other things. This chapter will explore the basics of object-oriented programming in Python.

Object-Oriented Programming abbreviated as OOP has several advantages over other design patterns. The development process is faster and cheaper, with great software maintainability. This, in turn, results in better software, which is also filled with new attributes and methods. The learning curve, is; however, complex. The idea might be complicated for newbies. In terms of computation, OOP is slower and consumes a lot of memory because more lines of code have been written.

Object-oriented programming relies on the important programming concept, which makes use of statements to change a program's state. It concentrates on illustrating how a program should operate. Examples of imperative programming languages are Java, C++, C, Ruby, and Python. This is different from declarative programming, which deals with the type of computer program that should achieve, without detailing how. Examples consist of database query languages such as XQuery and SQL.

OOP relies on the property of classes and objects. A class can be considered as a 'blueprint' for objects. These can feature their own characteristics and methods they execute.

Example of OOP

Take an example of a class Dog. Don't consider it as a specific dog or your own dog. We're describing what a dog is and what it can do in general. Dogs have an age and a name. These are instance properties. Dogs can also bark; this is a method.

When you discuss a certain dog, you would have an object in programming: an object is a class instance. This is the basic state on which object-oriented programming depends.

Now let's look at OOP in Python language.

Python is a powerful programming language that allows OOP. You will use Python language to define a class with properties and methods, which you will later call. Python has extra benefits than other languages. First, the language is dynamic and a high-level data type. This implies that development takes place faster than Java. It doesn't need the programmer to declare variable types and arguments. This makes Python easy to learn for beginners. Its code is more intuitive and readable.

It is important to remember that a class basically provides the structure. This is a blueprint that outlines how something needs to be defined. However, it doesn't offer any real content. For example, shape () class may specify the size and name of shapes, but it will not indicate the exact name of a shape.

You can view a class as a concept of how something should be executed.

Python Objects

Although the class is the blueprint, objects or instances are members of a given class. It's not a concept anymore. It's an actual shape, like a triangle with three sides.

Put differently; a class is like a questionnaire. It will define the required information. Once you complete the form, your actual copy is an instance of the class. It has original information relevant to you.

You can complete different copies to have multiple instances, but without the form, you'll be lost, not knowing the kind of information required. Therefore, before you can create individual objects, you need to define what is required by the class.

Defining a Class in Python

Below is a simple class definition in Python:

- Class Dog (object)

- Pass

When defining a class in Python, you begin with the class keyword to show that you're writing a class, then you follow it with the name of the class. In the above example, Dog is the name of the class.

The above class definition has the Python keyword pass; this is normally used as a placeholder where code will finally go. Why this keyword has been used is to avoid the code from throwing an error.

The object section enclosed in parentheses demonstrates the parent class that you're inheriting from. But this is no longer required in Python 3 because it's the implicit default.

Objects Attributes

All classes define objects, and all objects have properties known as attributes. The _init_ () method is used to specify an object's original properties by outlining their default value. This method requires at least one argument as the self-variable, which describes the object itself.

```python
class Dog:

    # Initializer / Instance Attributes
    def __init__(self, name, age):
        self.name = name
        self.age = age
```

In the following example, each dog has a unique name and age, which is critical to know, especially when you begin to define different dogs. Don't forget that the class is only defining the Dog, and not creating objects of individual dogs with unique names and ages.

Similarly, the self-variable also belongs to an instance of the class. Because class instance has different values, you can write Dog.name = name instead of self.name = name.

Class Attributes

While instance attributes are unique to every object, the characteristics of a class are the same for all instances. In this case, all dogs.

Methods

When you have attributes that belong to a class, you can proceed to define functions that will access the class attribute. These functions are referred to as methods. When you declare methods, you will want to provide the first argument to the method using a self-keyword.

For instance, you can define a class Snake, which contains the attribute name and the method change_name. The method change name will accept an argument new_name plus the keyword self.

Now, you can instantiate this class with a variable snake and change the name using the method change_name.

```
>>> # instantiate the class
>>> snake = Snake()

>>> # print the current object name
>>> print(snake.name)
python

>>> # change the name using the change_name method
>>> snake.change_name("anaconda")
>>> print(snake.name)
anaconda
```

Instance Attributes and the init Method

You can still provide the values for the attributes at runtime. This occurs by defining the attributes within the init method. Check out the example below:

```
class Snake:

    def __init__(self, name):
        self.name = name

    def change_name(self, new_name):
        self.name = new_name
```

Now you can proceed to directly define different attribute values for different objects.

So far, you know how to define Python classes, methods, and instantiate objects, and call instance methods. These skills will be useful when you want to solve complex problems.

With object-oriented programming, your code will increase in complexity as your program expands. You'll have different classes, objects, instance methods, and subclasses. You'll want to maintain your code and ensure it remains readable. To accomplish this, you will need to adhere to design patterns. These are principles that help a person to avoid bad design. Each represents a particular program that always reoccurs in OOP, and describes the solution to that problem, which can then be repeatedly used.

File Handling

Python provides a critical feature for reading data from the file and writing data into a file.

In most programming languages, all the values or data are kept in some volatile variables.

Since data will be stored in those variables during run-time only and will disappear once the program execution ends, therefore, it's better to save these data permanently using files.

Once you store data on a file, the next important

thing is its retrieval process because it's stored as bits of 1s and 0s, and in case the retrieval does not occur well, then it becomes completely useless, and that data is said to be corrupted.

How Python Handles Files?

If you're working in an extensive software application where they execute a massive amount of data, then we can't expect those data to be kept in a variable because variables are volatile.

Therefore, when you want to deal with these situations, the role of files will come into the picture.

Since files are non-volatile in nature, the data will remain permanently in a secondary device such as Hard Disk and using Python to deal with these files in your applications.

Do You Consider How Python Will Handle These Files?

Let's assume how normal people will deal with these files. If you want to read the data from a file or write the data into a file, then you need to open the file or create a new file if the file doesn't exist and then conduct the normal read/write operations, save the file and close it.

Similarly, the same operations are accomplished in Python with the help of in-built applications.

Types of Files in Python

There are two kinds of files:

1. Text files

2. Binary files

A file whose contents can be examined using a text editor is known as a text file. A text file refers to a sequence of ASCII characters. Python programs are examples of text files.

A binary file stores the data in the same manner as stored in the memory. The mp3 files, word documents are some of the examples of binary files. You cannot read a binary file using a text editor.

In Python language, file processing takes the following steps.

- Open a file that returns a filehandle.

- Use the handle to read or write action.

- Close the filehandle.

Before you perform a read or write operation to a file in Python, you must open it first. And as the read/write transaction finishes, you should close it to free the resources connected with the file.

Let's now look at each step in detail.

Access_mode: This is represented with an integer e.g read, write, and append. The default setting is the read-only <r>.

Buffering: The default value for buffering is 0. A zero value shows that buffering will not happen. If the value is 1, then the line buffering will happen while accessing the file. If it's more than 1, then the buffering action will proceed based on the size.

File_name: This is a string that represents the name of the file you want to access.

File open modes in Python language

<r>

<rb+>

<rb>

<w+>

<wb+>

<r+>

<w>

<wb>

Python File Object Properties

Once you call the Python open () function, it returns an object, which is the filehandle. Additionally, you need to understand that Python files have different features. And you can take advantage of the filehandle to list the features of a file it belongs.

Close a File in Python

It is good always to close a file when you finish your work. However, Python has a garbage collector to clean up the unused objects. However, you need to do it on your own instead of leaving it for the GC.

The Close Method

Python offers the <close ()> method to close a file.

When you close a file, the system creates resources allocated to it. And it's easy to accomplish.

Closing a file releases essential system resources. If you forgot to close the file, Python will do it automatically when the program ends, or the file object is no longer referenced inside the program. However, in case your program is large, and you're reading or writing multiple files that can consume a massive amount of resources on the system. If you continue opening new files carelessly, you might run out of resources.

CHAPTER - 7
DEVELOPMENT TOOLS

How to Run Python

Now before we start running our first python program, it is important that we understand how we can run python programs. Running or executing or deploying or firing a program simply means that we are making the computer process instructions/lines of codes.

For example, if the lines of codes (program) require the computer to display some message, then it should. The following are the ways or modes of running python programs. The interpreter is a special program that is installed when installing the Python package and helps convert text code into a language that the computer understands and can act on it (executing).

Immediate Mode

It is a way of running python programs that are not written in a file. We get into the immediate mode by typing the word python in the command line and which will trigger the interpreter to switch to immediate mode. The immediate mode allows typing of expressions directly, and pressing enter generates the output. The sign below is the Python prompt:

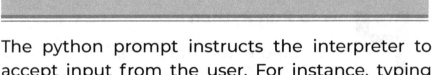

```
>>>
```

The python prompt instructs the interpreter to accept input from the user. For instance, typing 2+2 and pressing enter will display 4 as the output. In a way, this prompt can be used as a calculator. If you need to exit the immediate mode, type quit() or exit().

Now type 5 +3, and press enter, the output should be 8. The next mode is the Script Mode.

Script Mode

The script mode is used to run a python program written in a file; the file is called a script.

The scripts can be saved to external storage such as a disk for later use. All python scripts have the file extension .py, which implies that the filename ends with .py. An example is myFirstProg.py. We shall explain later how to write python scripts.

What is the IDE?

An IDE provides a convenient way of writing and running Python programs. One can also use text editors to create a python script file instead of an IDE by writing lines of codes and saving the file with a .py extension. However, using an IDE can simplify the process of writing and running Python programs. The IDEL present in the Python package is an example of an IDE with a graphical user interface and gets installed along with the Python language. The advantages of IDE include helping getting rid of repetitive tasks and simplify coding for beginners. IDE provides syntax highlighting, code hinting, and syntax checking, among other features. There also commercial IDE, such as the PyScripter IDE, that performs most of the mentioned functions.

The IDE is going to be important to what we are able to do inside of our language. You need to have some kind of IDE or environment in place in order to handle any of the coding. Without this, you will find that the programs will not work.

The good news is that the IDE is simple to install, and will not be too difficult to get to work with. And there are many Python IDE"s that you will be able to choose from. It often depends on the features and other add-ons that you would like to have with the environment that you choose.

Keep in mind that a few of these are going to cost a bit of money based on who designs them, and what kinds of features you find in them. You can choose whether those features are important to what you want to do or not.

If you are looking to keep costs down, while still ensuring that you get a good IDE that has all of the features and more that you need, you can go visit the www.python.org website. This will ensure, along with the Python download, that you get the IDE and all of the other files that you need to make coding in Python possible. And it will do all of this for free to help you keep costs down!

Your First Program in Python

The rest of the illustrations will assume you are running the python programs in a Windows environment.

- Start IDLE

- to the File menu and click New Window

- Type the following:

```
print ("Hello World!")
```

- On the File, menu clicks Save. Type the name of myProgram1.py

- Navigate to Run and click Run Module to run

the program.

The first program that we have written is known as the "Hello World!" and is used to not only provide an introduction to a new computer coding language but also test the basic configuration of the IDE. The output of the program is "Hello World!" Here is what has happened, the Print() is an inbuilt function; it is prewritten and preloaded for you, is used to display whatever is contained in the () as long as it is between the double-quotes. The computer will display anything written within the double-quotes.

Work to do: Now write and run the following python programs:

```
Print("I am now a Python Language Coder!")

Print("This is my second simple program!" )

Print("I love the simplicity of Python")

Print("I will display whatever is here in quotes such as owyhen2589gdbnz082")
```

Now we need to write a program with numbers, but before writing such a program, we need to learn something about Variables and Types.

Remember, python is object-oriented and it is not statically typed, which means we do not need to declare variables before using them or specify their type. Let us explain this statement; an object-oriented language simply means that the language supports viewing and manipulating real-life scenarios as groups with subgroups that can be linked and shared mimicking the natural order and interaction of things. Not all programming languages are object-oriented; for instance, Visual C programming language is not object-oriented. In programming, declaring variables means that we explicitly state the nature of the variable. The variable can be declared as an integer, long integer, short integer, floating integer, a string, or as a character, including if it is accessible locally or globally. A variable is a storage location that changes values depending on conditions.

For instance, number1 can take any number from 0 to infinity. However, if we specify explicitly that int number1 it then means that the storage location will only accept integers and not fractions, fortunately, or unfortunately, python does not require us to explicitly state the nature of the storage location (declare variables) as that is left to the python language itself to figure out that.

Before tackling types of variables and rules of writing variables, let us run a simple program to help us understand how to make this happen.

a. Start IDLE

b. Navigate to the File menu and click New Window

c. Type the following:

```
num1=4

num2=5

sum=num1+num2

print(sum)
```

d. On the File, menu clicks Save. Type the name of myProgram2.py

e. Navigate to Run and click Run Module to run the program.

The expected output of this program should be "9" without the double-quotes.

At this point, you are eager to understand what has just happened and why the print(sum) does not have double quotes like the first programs we wrote. Here is the explanation.

The first line num1=4 means that variable num1(our shortened way of writing number1, first number) has been assigned 4 before the program runs.

The second line num2=5 means that variable num2(our shortened way of writing number2, second number) has been assigned 5 before the program runs.

The computer interprets these instructions and stores the numbers given

The third line sum=num1+num2 tells the computer that takes whatever num1 has been given and add to whatever num2 has been given. In other terms, sum the values of num1 and num2.

The fourth line print(sum) means that display whatever sum has. If we put double quotes to sum, the computer will simply display the word sum and not the sum of the two numbers! Remember that cliché that computers are garbage in and garbage out. They follow what you give them!

Now let us try out three exercises involving numbers before we explain types of variables. Remember variables values vary, for instance, num1 can take 3, 8, 1562, 1.

Follow the steps of opening the Python IDE and do the following:

f. The output should be 54

```
num1=43

num2=11

sum=num1+num2

print(sum)
```

g. The output should be 167

```
num1=101
num2=66
sum=num1+num2
print(sum)
```

h. The output should be 28

```
num1=9
num2=19
sum=num1+num2
print(sum)
```

CHAPTER - 8

PROPER INSTALLATION

Installing Python (Windows)

Part of getting started with Python is installing the Python on your Windows. For the first step of the installation, you will need to download the installation package for your preferred version from this link below: https://www.python.org/downloads/

Visiting this link, you will be directed to a page. On that page, you will need to choose between the two latest versions for Python 2 and 3: Python 3.8.1 and Python 2.7.17.

In the other way round, if you are looking for a specific release, you can explore the page to find download links for earlier versions. Normally, you would opt to download the latest version, which is Python 3.8.1 –which was released on October 14, 2019 –or you download the latest version of Python

2, 2.7.17. However, the version you download must be because of the kind of project you want to do, compatibility, and support for updates.

Once you're finished with the download, you can proceed to installation by clicking on the downloaded .exe file. A standard installation has to incorporate pip, IDLE, and the essential documentation.

Installing Python (Mac)

If you're using a Mac, you can download the installation package from this link:

https://www.python.org/downloads/mac-osx/

The progression of learning is getting further into Python Programming Language. In reality, Python is an adaptable yet powerful language that can be used from multiple points of view. This just implies Python can be used intelligently when code or a declaration is to be tried on a line-by-line premise or when you're investigating its highlights. Incredibly, Python can be used in content mode, most particularly when you want to decipher a whole document of declarations or application program.

Working with Python, be that as it may, requires most extreme caution – particularly when you are drawing in or connecting with it. This caution is valid for each programming language as well. So as to draw in with Python intelligently, the Command Line window or the IDLE Development

Environment can be used.

Since you are an apprentice of either programming by and large or using Python, there will shift ventures on how you could connect with and cooperate with Python programming language. The following are basic highlights of activities for brisk cooperation with Python:

The Command-Line Interaction

Associating with the order line is the least difficult approach to work, as a novice, with Python. Python can simply be imagined by seeing how it functions through its reaction to each finished direction entered on the >>> brief. The Command-Line probably won't be the most favored commitment with Python; at the same time, throughout the years, it has demonstrated to be the easiest method to investigate how Python functions for learners.

Launching Python using the Command Line

If you're using macOS, GNU/Linux, and UNIX frameworks, you should run the Terminal tool to get to the command line. Then again, if you are using Windows, you can get to the Python order line by right-clicking on the Start menu and launching Windows PowerShell.

As directions on programming require a contribution of an order, when you need Python to do something for you, you will train it by entering directions that it knows about a similar yield. This is an adjustment in the order may give the ideal yield; be cautious.

With this, Python will make an interpretation of these directions to guidelines that your PC or gadget can comprehend and execute.

Let's take a look at certain guides to perceive how Python functions. Note that you can use the print order to print the all-inclusive program

"Heydays, Savants!"

1. Above all else, open Python's command line.

2. At that point, at the >>>prompt, type the accompanying (don't leave space among print and the section): print ("Heydays, Savants!")

3. Now, you should press enter so as to disclose to Python that you're finished with the direction. Promptly, the direction line window will show Heydays, Savants! In the interim, Python has reacted similarly as it has been told in the composed arrangement that it can relate with. Then again, to perceive how it will react wrongly when you request that it print a similar string using a wrong linguistic structure for the print order, type and enter the accompanying direction on the Python order brief: Print("Heydays, Savants!")

The outcome will be: Syntax error: invalid language structure

This is a case of what get when you use invalid or fragmented explanations. Note that Python is a case-touchy programming language, so at whatever point you misunderstand the message, it could be that you composed print with a capital letter. Obviously, there is a choice to print direction; you can simply type your announcement inside statements like this: "Primes, Savants!" Note that an announcement is the words you wish to show once the order is given; the words that can fit in are not confined to the model given here, however.

The most effective method to leave the Python order line

To exit from Python, you can type any of these commands: quit() or exit(). Subsequently, hold Control-Z and afterward press Enter; the Python should exit.

Your commonality with Python Programming ought to get fascinating now; there are still parts to learn, tolerance will satisfy.

The area of IDLE: Python's Integrated Development Environment (IDE)

A standout amongst the fascinating pieces of Python is the IDLE (Integrated Development and Learning Environment) apparatus. Despite the fact that this specific device is incorporated into Python's establishment bundle, you can download increasingly refined outsider IDEs as well. The IDLE instrument gives you access to an increasingly effective stage to compose your code and work engagingly with Python. To get to IDLE, you can experience a similar organizer where you found the direction line symbol or on the begin menu (as you've gained from order line collaboration). When you click on the IDLE symbol, you will be coordinated to the Python Shell window. This will take us to the segment on cooperation with the Python Shell Window.

Connecting with the Python Shell Window

When you're at the Python Shell Window, you will see a dropdown menu and a >>>prompt that resembles what you've found in the direction line window (the principal connection talked about). There is a specific IDLE's function of altering for the drawing in past order. Now, you will use a similar IDLE's altering menu to look back to your past directions, cut, copy, and glue past statements and, taking all things together, make any type of editing. Clearly, the IDLE is increasingly similar to a jump from the direction line association. Incredibly, in the menu dropdown of the Python Shell window are the accompanying menu things: File, Windows, Help, Shell, Options, Edit, and Debug. Every one of these menus has various functions. The Shell and Debug menus are used while making bigger projects as they give get highlights to the procedure. In any case, while the Shell menu gives you a chance to restart the shell or look the shell's log for the latest reset, Debug Menu has loads of valuable things for following the source record of an exemption and featuring the blundering line. With the Debugger option, you will most likely introduce an intelligent debugger window that will enable you to stop and look through the running projects on the Python. The Options menu of the window enables you to edit and set IDLE to suit your own Python working inclinations.

Moreover, at the Help menu, you are opened to choice Python Help and documentation.

Using the File Window menu, you will most likely make another document, open a module, open an old record, as well as spare your session through the essential things naturally made once you get to this menu. With the 'New File' alternative, you will almost certainly make codes you should simply to tap on it. When you have, you will be taken to another window with a straightforward and standard word processor where you can type or alter your code. You will see that the record is 'untitled' don't freeze; this is the underlying name of the document, which will change when you spare your code. One awesome thing about the File window menu is that refuse to have both the 'Shell' and 'Menu' choices together, so the bar changes just somewhat with the Shell Window. What happens is that in the Shell Window, two new Menus have been presented, to be specific: the Run and the Format menus. At whatever point you need to run the codes you have composed on the record window, the yield will be given on the Shell Window individually.

Toward the start of this area, you're informed that Python can be used in the Script Mode. How would you do this? The method of getting the outcome is very extraordinary at this point. When working in a content mode, the outcome you will get won't be programmed as in the manner you would in connecting with or associating mode. You should summon them out of your code. To get your yield on this mode, run the content or order it through the print() work inside your code.

To finish up this section, you've been taken through the essential two methods of the Python Programming Language; the drawing in or associating and the Script modes. Whatever the circumstance, realize that the fundamental change in that one outcome is getting dependent on order while the other is programmed.

CHAPTER - 9
DATA SCIENCE

Data Science and Its Significance

Data Science has come a long way from the past few years, and thus, it becomes an important factor in understanding the workings of multiple companies. Below are several explanations that prove data science will still be an integral part of the global market.

1. The companies would be able to understand their client in a more efficient and high manner with the help of Data Science. Satisfied customers form the foundation of every company, and they play an important role in their successes or failures. Data Science allows companies to engage with customers in the advance way and thus proves the product's improved performance and strength.

2. Data Science enables brands to deliver powerful and engaging visuals. That's one of the reasons

it's famous. When products and companies make inclusive use of this data, they can share their experiences with their audiences and thus create better relations with the item.

3. Perhaps one Data Science's significant characteristics are that its results can be generalized to almost all kinds of industries, such as travel, health care, and education. The companies can quickly determine their problems with the help of Data Science, and can also adequately address them

4. Currently, data science is accessible in almost all industries, and nowadays, there is a huge amount of data existing in the world, and if used adequately, it can lead to victory or failure of any project. If data is used properly, it will be important in the future to achieve the product 's goals.

5. Big data is always on the rise and growing. Big data allows the enterprise to address complicated Business, human capital, and capital management problems effectively and quickly using different resources that are built routinely.

6. Data science is gaining rapid popularity in every other sector and therefore plays an important role in every product's functioning and performance. Thus, the data scientist's role is also enhanced as they will conduct an essential

function of managing data and providing solutions to particular issues.

7. Computer technology has also affected the supermarket sectors. To understand this, let's take an example the older people had a fantastic interaction with the local seller. Also, the seller was able to meet the customers' requirements in a personalized way. But now this attention was lost due to the emergence and increase of supermarket chains. But the sellers are able to communicate with their customers with the help of data analytics.

8. Data Science helps companies build that customer connection. Companies and their goods will be able to have a better and deeper understanding of how clients can utilize their services with the help of data science.

Data Technology Future: Like other areas are continually evolving, the importance of data technology is increasingly growing as well. Data science impacted different fields. Its influence can be seen in many industries, such as retail, healthcare, and education. New treatments and technologies are being continually identified in the healthcare sector, and there is a need for quality patient care. The healthcare industry can find a solution with the help of data science techniques that helps the patients to take care of. Education is another field where one can clearly see the advantage of data science. Now the new innovations like phones and tablets have become an essential characteristic of the educational system. Also, with the help of data science, the students are creating greater chances, which leads to improving their knowledge.

Data Structures

A data structure may be selected in computer programming or designed to store data for the purpose of working with different algorithms on it. Every other data structure includes the data values, data relationships, and functions between the data that can be applied to the data and information.

Features of data structures

Sometimes, data structures are categorized according to their characteristics. Possible functions are:

- Linear or non-linear: This feature defines how the data objects are organized in a sequential series, like a list or in an unordered sequence, like a table.

- Homogeneous or non-homogeneous: This function defines how all data objects in a collection are of the same type or of different kinds.

- Static or dynamic: This technique determines to show to assemble the data structures. Static data structures at compilation time have fixed sizes, structures, and destinations in the memory. Dynamic data types have dimensions, mechanisms, and destinations of memory that may shrink or expand depending on the application.

Data structure Types

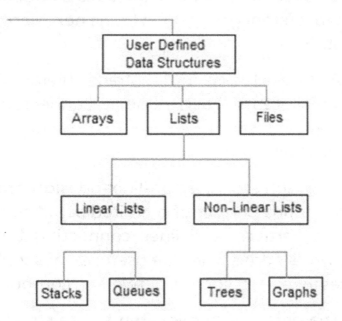

Types of the data structure are determined by what sorts of operations will be needed or what kinds of algorithms will be implemented. This includes:

Arrays: An array stores a list of memory items at adjacent locations. Components of the same category are located together since each element's position can be easily calculated or accessed. Arrays can be fixed in size or flexible in length.

Stacks: A stack holds a set of objects in linear order added to operations. This order may be past due in first out (LIFO) or first-out (FIFO).

Queues: A queue stores a stack-like selection of elements; however, the sequence of activity can only be first in the first out. Linked lists: In a linear order, a linked list stores a selection of items. In a linked list, every unit or node includes a data item as well as a reference or relation to the next element in the list.

Trees: A tree stocks an abstract, hierarchical collection of items. Each node is connected to other nodes and can have several sub-values, also known as a child.

Graphs: A graph stores a non-linear design group of items. Graphs consist of a limited set of nodes, also called vertices, and lines connecting them, also known as edges. They are useful for describing processes in real life, such as networked computers.

Tries: A tria or query tree is often a data structure that stores strings as data files, which can be arranged in a visual graph.

Hash tables: A hash table or hash chart is contained in a relational list that labels the keys to variables. A hash table uses a hashing algorithm to transform an index into an array of containers containing the desired item of data. These data systems are called complex because they can contain vast quantities of interconnected data. Examples of primal, or fundamental, data structures are integer, float, boolean, and character.

Utilization of data structures

Data structures are generally used to incorporate the data types in physical forms. This can be interpreted into a wide range of applications, including a binary tree showing a database table. Data structures are used in the programming languages to organize code and information in digital storage. Python databases and dictionaries, or JavaScript array and objects, are popular coding systems used to gather and analyze data. Also, data structures are a vital part of effective software design. Significance of Databases Data systems is necessary to effectively handle vast volumes of data, such as data stored in libraries, or indexing services.

Accurate data configuration management requires memory allocation identifier, data interconnections, and data processes, all of which support the data structures. In addition, it is important to not only use data structures but also to select the correct data structure for each assignment.

Choosing an unsatisfactory data structure could lead to slow running times or disoriented code. Any considerations that need to be noticed when choosing a data system include what type of information should be processed, where new data will be put, how data will be organized, and how much space will be allocated for the data.

How significant is Python for Data Science?

- Efficient and simple to use—Python is considered a tool for beginners, and any student or researcher with only basic understanding could start working on it. Time and money spent debugging codes and constraints on different project management are also minimized. The time for code implementation is less compared to other programming languages such as C, Java, and C #, which makes developers and software engineers spend far more time working on their algorithms.

- Library Choice—Python offers a vast library and machine learning and artificial intelligence database. Scikit Learn, TensorFlow, Seaborn, Pytorch, Matplotlib, and many more are among the most popular libraries.

- Scalability—It gives flexibility in solving problems that can't be solved with other computer languages. Many companies use it to develop all sorts of rapid techniques and systems.

- Visual Statistics and Graphics—Python provides a number of visualization tools. The Matplotlib library provides a reliable framework on which those libraries such as gg plot, pandas plotting, PyTorch, and others are developed. These services help create graphs, plot lines ready for the Web, visual layouts, etc.

How Python is used for Data Science

First phase—First of all, we need to learn and understand what form a data takes. If we perceive data to be a huge Excel sheet with columns and crows lakhs, then perhaps you should know what to do about that? You need to gather information into each row as well as column by executing some operations and searching for a specific type of data. Completing this type of computational task can consume a lot of time and hard work. Thus, you can use Python's libraries, such as Pandas and Numpy, that can complete the tasks quickly by using parallel computation.

Second phase—The next hurdle is to get the data needed. Since data is not always readily accessible to us, we need to dump data from the network as needed. Here the Python Scrap and brilliant Soup libraries can enable us to retrieve data from the internet.

Third phase—We must get the simulation or visual presentation of the data at this step. Driving perspectives gets difficult when you have too many figures on the board. The correct way to do that is to represent the data in graph form, graphs, and other layouts. The Python Seaborn and Matplotlib libraries are used to execute this operation.

Fourth phase—The next stage is machine-learning, which is massively complicated computing. It includes mathematical tools such as the probability, calculus, and matrix operations of columns and rows over lakhs. With Python's machine learning library Scikit-Learn, all of this will become very simple and effective.

CHAPTER - 10

LEARNING MACHINE

Computers have become an integral part of modern-day operations in almost every sphere of life. Teaching computers how to operate and progressively improve on functionality takes different approaches. The types of machine learning are categorized into taxonomies depending on the underlying problems or the anticipated outcomes. These types of machine learning allow the computer to learn patterns and regularities that are useful across a variety of business and health-related fields in the modern world. The following are some of the types of learning algorithms useful in the process of machine learning.

Supervised Learning

Supervised learning occurs where the algorithms create a function that maps raw data into desired outputs. Supervised learning is one of the most common paradigms for machine learning. It is easy to comprehend. The process of implementation of supervised learning may be achieved through systems from the training dataset. The training data or examples contain more than one input and the desired output. The output is also known as a regulatory signal, which is represented within the mathematical model. An array of vectors represents the training example. When provided with data in the form of illustrations, the algorithms may be useful in the prediction of each name. Forecasting takes place in the process of giving a response on whether the answers were right or wrong. The approach allows the algorithms a chance to learn to make approximations over time that allow for the distinction between the labels and the examples. The method makes supervised learning a common option in the process of finding solutions...

The most common supervised learning approaches include classification and regression. In the case of classification, the use of supervised learning occurs where the outputs may have restrictions on a fixed number of values. Classification typically deals with the identification in a given data set with a view to linking new observations into such categories. On the other hand, the use of regression occurs when the outputs have a wide range of numerical values within a given subset. The goal in both examples is to ensure that machine learning utilizes a fixed set of training examples to make the necessary comparisons on how similar or different a collection of data may be in a given subset. The optimal scenarios in such data sets ensure that the algorithms can determine the class labels for all the unseen occurrences within such a subgroup.

Unsupervised Learning

Machines learning may occur through unsupervised cluster analysis. The approach involves using a set of data that is made up of inputs, which is necessary for the development of a structure. The clustering of data points is an example of unsupervised learning. Unlike in the case of supervised learning, the test data in unsupervised learning does not have labels and is not within a specific classification. Unsupervised learning does not respond to feedback but instead focuses on the commonalities. The method seeks to identify the possibility of commonalities in a given set of data and use these commonalities to develop a pattern. Essentially, this means that the goal is to task a computer with learning how to do something without providing a logical approach to achieve this task. The unsupervised approach is, therefore, more complicated and more complex than the supervised process. This method means using a reward approach to affirm success in the achievement of the tasks without necessarily providing explicit instructions on how to achieve the set goals.

The purpose of the unsupervised approach is more aligned towards the decision-making process as opposed to the mere classification of these data. Unsupervised learning trains the agent to act or respond to tasks based on the reward system or punishment built over time. A computer gradually learns how to navigate past commands without having prior information on the anticipated outcomes. This approach may be time-consuming and tedious. But unsupervised learning can be powerful because it operates from the point of trial and error, which may produce discoveries. Unsupervised learning does not consider any pre-classified information and therefore works from an aspect of the invention.

The unsupervised learning approach is critical in a world where most of the data sets in the world are unlabeled. This indisputable reality means that having intelligent algorithms that can utilize terabytes of unlabeled data and make sense of such information is critical. In the future, there will be different instances where unsupervised learning will become a crucial area of focus. Recommender systems will be a vital area where unsupervised learning will be applicable in the future. The recommender system allows for a distinct link to relationships, which makes it easy to categorize and suggest content based on shared likes.

Reinforcement Learning

Reinforcement learning is useful when the exact models are unrealistic because they rarely assume knowledge of an accurate mathematical model. The approach focuses on how machines should operate to maximize some aspects of cumulative rewards. In modern research, the application of reinforcement learning is observed from a behavioural psychology point of view. The method thus functions through interacting with the immediate environment. As we noted earlier, supervised learning operates based on existing examples. The user of interaction with the situation in the case of reinforcement learning indicates a difference between the two approaches.

The application of reinforcement learning in the field of Artificial Intelligence is an indication of the ability of the machines to learn and adjust to new tasks through interactions with the immediate environment. The algorithms adapt to taking specific action based on the observation of the contextual setting. The pattern of behavioural reaction to environmental stimuli is an indication of the process of learning that has become synonymous with artificial intelligence. Every action in reinforcement learning has a direct implication of the operational context, and this reaction provides an opportunity for the machine to receive feedback, which is critical in the process of learning. Reinforcement learning tends to rely on time-dependent sequences or labels. The results in the case of reinforcement learning depend on the connection between the agent and the environmental context. The agent is then given a set of tasks that have a direct implication on the environment. The method then approves a specific reinforcement signal, which provides negative or positive feedback depending on the job and the anticipated result.

Semi-supervised Machine Learning

The use of semi-supervised learning algorithms is essential, where there is a small amount of labelled data and enormous amounts of unlabelled data. The method utilizes the combination of both labelled and unlabelled data. The programmer, therefore, uses both data types to identify patterns. The deduced models become the basis on which relationships target variables, and the data examples become easy to identify and analyse. The approach refers to semi-supervised learning because it utilizes data from labelled and unlabelled examples and still makes sense out of this information. Semi-supervised learning is, therefore, a hybridization of supervised and unsupervised learning approaches. Semi-structured data is used in this case because it does not obey the formal structuring of data models. The tags and other indicators used in the semi-supervised approach aids in the separation of semantic elements. This is essential when there lack enough examples to develop an accurate model. Semi-structured models often make critical sense when there is a lack of adequate resources and limited capacity to increase the available data examples.

The approach allows for the labelling process of the defined data; then, it uses the trained model to classify the other data based on the specific model. In some instances, you may find situations where you have a wide range of data with a known outcome, yet also have another set of data that is unidentified. The use of semi-supervised machine learning allows the process to utilize the known data models to build a sequence that can be effective in the course of making labels for the rest of the data sets. As a result, when compared to other models, this approach provides the best option because it is time-saving and also reduces drastically the overall resources used towards achieving the intended outcome.

The creation of an appropriate function when using semi-supervised approaches may be a critical solution in a modern setting where unlabelled data is likely to supersede labelled data in the process of classification. The use of semi-supervised methods in spam identification and detection from standard messages is the most realistic example in the modern world. The use of human knowledge to sieve through such messages would otherwise be impossible to achieve. Using semi-supervised techniques helps in resolving the high dimensionality concern that often affects the process of classification.

CONCLUSION

You're on your way to work listening to your favorite Spotify playlist and scrolling through your Instagram feed. Once you arrive at the office, you head over to the coffee machine, and while waiting for your daily boost, you check your Facebook notifications. Finally, you head to your desk, take a sip of coffee, and you think, "Hey, I should Google to learn what Python is used for." At this point, you realize that every technology you just used has a little bit of Python in it.

Python is used in nearly everything, whether we are talking about a simple app created by a startup company or a giant corporation like Google. Let's go through a brief list of all the ways you can use Python.

In conclusion, Python and big data provide one of the strongest capabilities in computational terms on the platform of big data analysis. If this is your first time at data programming, Python will be a much easier language to learn than any other and is far more user-friendly.

And so, we've come to the end of this book, which was meant to give you a taste of data analysis techniques and visualization beyond the basics using Python. Python is a wonderful tool to use for data purposes, and I hope this guide stands you in good stead as you go about using it for your purposes.

I have tried to go more in-depth in this book, give you more information on the fundamentals of data science, along with lots of useful, practical examples for you to try out.

Please read this guide as often as you need to and don't move on from a chapter until you fully understand it. And do try out the examples included – you will learn far more if you actually do it rather than just reading the theory.

This was just an overview to recap on what you learned in the first book, covering the datatypes in pandas and how they are used. We also looked at cleaning the data and manipulating it to handle missing values and do some string operations.

There are a lot of other coding languages out there that you are able to work with, but Python is one of the best that works for most beginner programmers, providing the power and the ease of use that you are looking for when you first get started in this kind of coding language. This guidebook took the time to explore how Python works, along with some of the different types of coding that you can do with it.

In addition to seeing a lot of examples of how you can code in Python and how you can create some of your programs in this language, we also spent some time looking at how to work with Python when it comes to the world of machine learning, artificial intelligence, and data analysis. These are topics and parts of technology that are taking off, and many programmers are trying to learn more about it. And with the help of this guidebook, you will be able to handle all of these, even as a beginner in Python.

When you are ready to learn more about how to work with the Python coding language and how you can make sure that you can even use Python along with data analysis, artificial intelligence, and machine learning, make sure to check out again this guidebook to help you get started.